MW00899832

Baltimore Rock & Roll

True Stories from the Breathing City

Rock on!

Rebecca Schuman

Rebecca Schuman

To my parents, for giving me their old records,
to Cameron Crowe, who got me started,
and to Baltimore.

Text copyright © 2017 Rebecca Schuman

All rights reserved. No portion of this book may be reproduced in any form without permission from the publisher, except as permitted by U.S. copyright law.

ISBN-13: 978-1542326971
ISBN-10: 1542326974

Jacket photograph by Stuart Zolotorow

"If you truly dig what you are doing, if you lay it out that way, nobody can not respond. That's what rock and roll is; it's relentless."

Cass Elliot

"Music can change the world because it can change people."

Bono

Liner Notes

At fourteen years old, Baltimore resident Stephen Oshins decided he wanted to be exactly like Jim Morrison. He decided this at a 1967 Doors concert in New Haven, Connecticut, just before Morrison was forcibly arrested on the stage, and right after he started writhing on the ground, foaming at the mouth as handcuffs were snapped around his wrists. Moments earlier, Morrison had been ranting about a misunderstanding with the police backstage. His long tirade was sprinkled with colorful language, poetic in a distinctly Jim Morrison way, as he taunted the officers in the crowd below. Oshins was less than a foot from where the police jumped onto the stage set. And long after Morrison left the concert in a police car, the crowd taking to the streets to riot the unfairness of it all, Oshins still knew, he wanted to be exactly like Jim Morrison.

Rock 'n' roll is cult-like in its allure, underdog in its rebellion, and everything in context. While there's no one thing that can really place the core of the music, everyone can recognize how it has fit into their lives, memories shaped around soundtracks and album release dates, best-night-of-my-life concerts.

That's where the question comes in: is rock 'n' roll just that? A memory? The music that was once an adage for the young is the history of an aging generation. Rock 'n' roll was never meant to mature. Never meant to turnover gracefully, to call it a night. The Who's somewhat morbid line, "Hope I die before I get old," ("My Generation") is purposefully naive, caught in a wildly stuttering tune that dances around death and celebrates youth. And despite its seeming simplicity, the song goes beyond its required job, reminding us how rock 'n' roll reaches maximum power in impulsivity. Pride and spirit swirl together in a flurry that lasts a little over three minutes. Every time the song is played, that same flurry resonates, no matter the age of the listener.

One of the best things about the music, I've come to find, is the people. Not only would the music not exist without them—musicians, fans, journalists, photographers—these people are the driving force of the story. The narrative of rock 'n' roll is a series of segments, millions of them, that have been pieced together over the years. Anyone who was there will tell you, gladly, of the time they met Mick Jagger on vacation, or saw George Harrison live in concert. The world that was happening behind the music is still known today because people can't stop talking about it. And why would they? Rock 'n' roll was and is so far removed from the mundanity of the everyday that even *barely* close encounters were enough sometimes. Going to concerts was thrill-seeking, if just for one night, you could be a part of something else, something bigger.

The music lives on best through the fans. And this is a book made by the fans, for the fans, for everyone who remembers, and for everyone who wants to remember more. I did my best to gather as much information as possible, but, who knows how many stories remain buried?

When I first began this project, I only knew I wanted to write about the power of rock 'n' roll. Baltimore wasn't even in the picture for a good several months. As a Baltimore native and lifelong resident, my personal ties run deep. I found that my local interviews were weaving together an entirely unexpected subplot: turns out, more often than not, Baltimore was in the middle of things, including all things rock 'n' roll. Local Baltimore bands made it big, major musicians performed rare and impromptu gigs in underground bars, all within the expanse of the city. It was even more exciting to me to understand that Jimi Hendrix performed thirty minutes from my house, Eric Clapton down the road from my high school. Right here in my hometown, the Grateful Dead broke their own record, performing their longest recorded song, "The Other One" in 1972, coming in at an impressive forty minutes total.

My mother tells me that people who are born and raised in Baltimore tend to stay. She still remembers the old neighborhoods of her elementary school friends, and can point out the individual houses while driving. Baltimore is a cornerstone of memories for most residents. It makes sense that the music lives on through the city, as well. My dad recalls Hammerjacks with the same fondness he usually reserves for an Orioles win. To many, the Royal Farms Arena will always be the flashy new Baltimore Civic Center.

While interviewing for this book, I wanted to capture each memory and hold it down permanently in a way the buildings, streets, and people of Baltimore won't always be. The stories range from the blues, to Beatlemania, to the long, strange trip that was Woodstock, all from a distinctly Baltimore perspective. Interviews with photographers, history professors, activists, and producers join together to explain why it is we still listen to the music all these years later and all the years to come. I wanted this book to be like a record. You can pick it up at any page and fall into the world of Baltimore's rock story. Every track can stand on its own, but together is a perspective of a city with a lot to say.

Contents

Britain Invades Baltimore

"We were down, we needed a shot of cultural speed, something high, fast, loud and superficial to fill the gap; we needed a fling after the wake."

~Lester Bangs, 1970s music critic

On September 13, 1964, The Beatles descended on Baltimore like gods. It was a one-day stop, the twentieth city on their first American tour, but still only months after their historic appearance on the Ed Sullivan Show in February. The Beatles were coming, and everyone in Baltimore was going to know it.

Fans flocked to the streets around the Holiday Inn on Lombard Street where John, Paul, George, and Ringo were staying on the hotel's tenth floor. Teenage girls barricaded the entranceways, umbrellas slick with rain only reaffirming their dedication to catch just a glimpse. About two hundred city police officers stood guard, and for good reason.

The Beatles never had the opportunity for mystique other bands and musicians later strove for. Before the show, the boys were subjected to a series of press conferences and interviews with reporter Larry Kane and various others, questions ranging from setlist choices to weirdest gift from a fan (to which John replied: "I once received a bra . . . with 'I love John Lennon' embroidered on it. I thought it was pretty original. I didn't keep it, mind you—it didn't fit.") Journalists were mostly baffled by Beatlemania, unable to fully comprehend the teenage girl mindset, leaving conferences unimpressed with the long hair and rumpled, tieless suits.

In contrast, by the time of the concert, 26,000 fans flew screaming into the opened doors of the Baltimore Civic Center across the street from the Holiday Inn, drowning out the intercom speaker which warned, "Do not run into the building, walk." The band successfully made it across the street to the stage after a mad dash to their limousine, although it was a close call. And even with the high level security, fans weren't about to be deterred. Two girls attempted to deliver themselves to the concert in a large box marked, "Beatles Fan Mail." A Ringo fan smuggled her phone number inside the Beatles' dressing room.

The two concerts themselves were quick, a total of twelves songs pushed through one after the other like musical chain smoking. The first notes of "Twist and Shout" were muffled by the swelling hysteria of the audience, fans jumping up from their seats, grabbing their hair in their hands. Baltimore photographer Morton Tadder recalled in an interview, "When Beatles Paul said 'Thank you very much,' and kicked up a leg a meter or so, it was so pure, so true, so honest Paul that some of the most devout cried real tears."

Patricia Danoff didn't see the Beatles at the Civic Center in 1964 during their first tour in America. She did, however, catch them on their last tour in 1966 at the Robert. F. Kennedy Memorial Stadium (then named the D.C. Stadium) when she was a sophomore in college. "It was a few days after John Lennon made the crack about how the Beatles are more popular than Jesus Christ. There were protests by Christian groups outside of the stadium," says Danoff. Despite the clash, Danoff recalls the screams and the fans trying to rush the stage, business as usual for any Beatles concert. After all, who needed Jesus Christ when there was the Beatles?

It made sense that 1964 America found it easier to pray to the Beatles than to God, or even to Elvis. The clean-shaven boys looked young up close, and from the audience they were practically children, angelic faces singing innocent rhymes, "I wanna hold your hand." The 1960s opened to a grieving nation. If JFK

2

was a lifesize statue of American ideals and optimism, his death was a shot in the face to it all. The easy doo-wop and pop that then dominated American music was too reminiscent of the pure, unsullied nation of before. And we didn't want it. Our sound was grappling between Little Richard's "Good Golly Miss Molly" and The Beach Boys' "Surfin'" with no real in between. The country was lost, and our sound reflected just that. We needed an outside source, something foreign, hip, new—a distraction.

A large chunk of the British Invasion was, as music critic Lester Bangs explained, more about mood than music. The Beatles paved the way for even more Beatles, like Herman's Hermits, whose sugary sweet sound and baby-faced frontman, Peter Noone, kept spirits high. The success of Herman's Hermits is often downplayed by their perky song titles and fan demographic even younger than the so-called 'teeny-boppers.' But the simplicity of "Something Tells Me I'm Into Something Good" makes it feel as though the quaint tune has always been there, readymade to be heard and loved. Noone's grin and "Who, me?" stage act pulls through during performances of "Mrs. Brown, You've Got a Lovely Daughter."

Of course, there was another end to the spectrum. We Americans thought we were discovering a new world of music, the ocean between the continents like another universe, supplying mystical secrets we never would have unearthed on our own. That would have been true if half of the music of the Invasion wasn't influenced by our own backyards, i. e. the blues.

One of the most frequently told stories of rock 'n' roll involves two boys at a Dartford train station with a Chuck Berry and a Muddy Waters record. The tale goes like this: Keith Richards and Mick Jagger were friends during early childhood until Jagger's family moved to a wealthier neighborhood later on. Jagger never really saw Richards after the move, excluding the occasion Jagger bought an ice cream cone from him one summer when Richards was intent on earning a few bucks. But of all places, in a train station in Dartford, when Richards, his Hofner cutaway electric guitar in hand, approached Jagger (or Jagger approached Richards? No one really knows for sure) and saw those two records under his arm, everything else just sort of fell into place. In an excited letter to his grandmother following the meeting, Richards wrote, "The guy on the station, he is called Mick Jagger and ... is the greatest R&B singer this side of the Atlantic and I don't mean maybe." Thus, British-American-everybody blues was born, white kids in America with little idea of how this music came to be. How were they to know that this music had been thriving in America all along, and that it took the British to show them what they already had?

The blues side of the British Invasion was no doubt grittier. While there was a clear tone set with every new release from Gerry and the Pacemakers, other bands like The Animals, Manfred Mann, and Cream were more intent on following the traditional sounds of John Lee Hooker, Howlin' Wolf. When Brian Jones formed the Rolling Stones, "rock 'n' roll" wasn't in the picture. He snatched the name from the Muddy Waters song, "Rollin' Stone," determined that blues and blues alone would be the band's success. The Stone's rebellious image was more a marketing scheme than anything else. Not a Beatles fan? You're in luck: here are the *anti*-Beatles!

Overall, the music was a binding force, tying together a floundering generation that could easily have been lost to the anxieties and hopelessness of the older folks. Of course, people who are in mourning generally aren't so interested in what's next. Danoff remembers her parents' reaction to Bob Dylan, a singer who, while not British, invaded America in his own right in the early 1960s with tragically cynical eyes that questioned the nation at its core. "I remember my father wrote in pen on the front of one of [Dylan's] albums, 'I can't believe this guy is for real,' or something like that. I remember thinking that he had defaced a piece of my property," Danoff says with a laugh.

And as the bond of the boomers grew through the music, the gap between the parents only seemed to widen. "They were amused. They couldn't understand why we liked [these bands]," explains Danoff. Amused was one reaction to rock 'n' roll. The other reaction was more severe, looking to satanic allusions for an explanation. The idea of "devil's music" originates from old school superstition of the black community. The blues was "blue-collar," working class, unlike gospel. However, the blues was and is a definite layer of black culture and history. No one was ever going to stop playing or listening. The taboo may have even encouraged listeners.

As people like Elvis began blending blues with rock, the music took on even stronger opposition. Reverend Jimmie Snow believed that rock 'n' roll was a cause of "juvenile delinquency." "Why I believe that is because I know how it feels when you sing it, I know what it does to you, and I know of the evil feeling that you feel when you sing it!" Snow gestured passionately during a sermon. While adults were furiously checking records for signs of devilish manipulations, the rest of young America wasn't looking for answers.

White America didn't know much about the taboo in the African American community, let alone understand its significance. It wasn't until those guys from the British country-side came barreling over with this "new sound" that they even considered it. It took another country to sell them what they already had. Before the Beatles' impact hit, Sam Phillips of Sun Records said at one point, "If I could ever find a white boy who could sing like a black man, I'd make a million dollars." He was in luck.

Who Are You?

Patricia Danoff

In 1975, Patricia Danoff and her husband, Jerry, went to an Emerson, Lake and Palmer concert.

We saw them at the Washington D. C. Capital Centre. And the thing we remember about it is that it was so loud, we ended up holding our fingers in our ears practically the whole time. It was hurting our ears, it was so loud!

Favorite Band: The Beatles

Favorite Song: "Octopus's Garden" by The Beatles

Why I relate to classic rock:

I guess probably because of peer pressure. Everybody else was doing it, and so you wanted to be a part of the group. Somebody says, "Do you have the new album?" [and] you wanted to make sure you had it.

How the Boomers Rose to Power

The United States Census Bureau concludes that there were a total of 76 million births between 1946 and 1964, an unprecedented amount in such a short expanse of time. And as a result, the population, well, *boomed*.

Several different factors went into play in causing the increase. Legislation passed before and during the war made it easier for veterans to transition back into their lives without economic stress. The Servicemen's Readjustment Act was also signed into law in 1944, which helped returning soldiers pay for higher education, medical necessities, loans for new homes, job training, etc. The security and all-around joyous mood over a hard-won war powered consumerism, which led to a doubling in national income during the mid-1950s. With increased economic growth, the standard of living thrived, America's middle class about sixty percent of the overall population. Settling down with a family was inevitable at this point.

And the consumerism didn't end with televisions and automobiles. Boomers single-handedly carried the entire blue jeans market on their shoulders, along with other clothing lines and, of course, records. By the 1970s, industries were finally beginning to cater to the Boomer's tastes. Things weren't all white picket fences for long. Music became the highest grossest industry of the decade. Which was a difficult pill to swallow for some. The late 60s thrived on free concerts, and enough love to go around. By the 70s, most record companies and labels took notice: there was money to be made here.

On the Road Again

Major Bands That Passed Through Baltimore

The Animals (1962-1966): The Animals performed at the Baltimore Civic Center on July 30 in 1966. The group shared the bill with Herman's Hermits, and the sets lasted around twenty to thirty minutes. The band had already decided to break up that past May, but went through with the tour anyway because of technicalities in their contracts.

The Beatles (1960-1970): The Beatles performed at the Baltimore Civic Center on September 13, 1964 during their first tour in America. They played two concerts, each one lasting under an hour.

Cream (1966-1968): Cream also performed at the Baltimore Civic Center on November 3, 1968 during their "farewell" tour of the states. Their concert poster for the event describes the group as "the most important, controversial pop stars in the world."

Herman's Hermits (1964-1971): Herman's Hermits played at the Baltimore Civic Center alongside The Animals July, 1966. They returned during the third United States tour on August 11, 1967.

The Moody Blues (1964-): The Moody Blues opened for Cream at the Baltimore Civic Center on November 3 in 1968.

The Rolling Stones (1962-): The Rolling Stones performed at the Baltimore Civic Center on November 12, 165, June 26, 1966, and again on November 26, 1969. The 1969 concert album for Baltimore, *Devil's Disciple* reveals that Jagger sings a quick "Hey Jude" during the outro of "Sympathy for the Devil," appropriate considering the Beatles' break-up just before this tour. Part of this performance was also used on their live album, *Get Yer Ya-Ya's Out.*

The Who (1964-): The Who came to the Baltimore Civic Center August 11th, 1967. They played only one show and didn't come on the stage until around 8:30 pm. They returned in 1969 for a performance at the Merriweather Post Pavilion on May 5th, their opening band the young, and, at that point, fairly unknown Led Zeppelin. Most of the "Tommy" album was performed live, and little bits of Moon's drumsticks were flying out into the audience" when they went into "Magic Bus." For a final kicker, Townshend concluded the show by breaking his guitar over his head, not that unusual for a Who concert.

The Yardbirds (1963-1968): The Yardbirds performed at the Baltimore Civic Center during the weekend of September 10-11 in 1966. The event was hosted by WCAO disc jockeys. This was Jimmy Page's first North American tour with the group.

The Buddy Deane Show

In a sense, Baltimore has always been its own epicenter. That's why when the rest of the nation tuned in for *American Bandstand*, Baltimore responded with *The Buddy Deane Show*, an energetic, ahead-of-its-times program that asked kids and parents alike some pretty heavy questions, all while bringing some of the best, undiscovered music to the city.

The show began in 1957 on WJZ-TV as a swinging romp with teenagers dancing to live performances in the studio. Often, local bands were propelled to fame through the show. Bill Haley and His Comets gave a quick version of "Rock Around the Clock" on the show in 1959, a full year before it was formally released to the public. It was Deane who emphasized the importance of *good* music, not just fun music. Deane recalled in an interview, "One guy who had a record shop up on Pennsylvania Avenue told me, 'Never waste a groove'. It made sense to me. If it's not a hit, don't play it." It was this sort of thinking that led almost every major performing artist to play on the show at some point in its run.

Originally from Arkansas, Deane first came to Baltimore in 1951 as a morning disc jockey for WITH radio. He worked his way up, appearing as a jockey at larger concerts, until WITH DJ, Joel Chaseman, helped Deane move into his own slot on television. Eventually, this little show went on to win "The Best Daytime Show in America" award in 1962.

The show wasn't just a claim to fame for bands. Deane turned high schoolers into local celebrities overnight. Together these lucky kids formed The

Committee, turning out dances like "The Madison" and "the mashed potato" six times a week at three o'clock in the afternoon. Buddy Deane Show dancer, Frani Hahn remembers, "[W]e would go downtown shopping and we'd stop in at Read's Drug Store and have Cokes, and people came up for our autographs!"

By the mid 1960s, calls to integrate the show were too loud to ignore. The Committee held meetings as protests swept the city, but the ultimate decision was that of the Committee's parents--integrated dancing on television was a no-go. The final episode aired 4 January, 1964. The show's run is immortalized in the 1988 film, *Hairspray*, written and directed by self-proclaimed Buddy Deane mega-fan, John Waters.

While Buddy Deane enraptured the city for almost seven years, the 1960s were barreling in fast and at full force. Perhaps marking the clearest transition between the times was when Deane introduced the Beatles on stage at the Baltimore Civic Center, almost like a handshake between the two decades.

Baltimore's Immigrant Song

Before the Beatles invaded, and before the blues was situated, there was just Baltimore. But then again, it was never *just* Baltimore. First founded in 1729, Baltimore started out as more of a village, surrounded mostly by wheat and tobacco fields. Slaves were the primary resource for labor in Maryland, so Baltimore's population grew as its economy and industry grew, capitalizing on the free work source. The slave trade as a whole relied heavily on the city, and by 1790, there were more than twice as many slaves as free blacks. When Baltimore drifted from agriculture, slaves and free black men were assigned to the maritime business as joiners, caulkers, carvers, sailmakers, and plumbers.

After the War of 1812, a large wave of German immigrants flooded the city, escaping the War of the Sixth Coalition, the last remnants of the French Revolutionary Wars. Mostly, these people were avoiding the conscription into the Royal Prussian Army.

By the 1820s, the port of Baltimore was the second largest gateway for immigrants next to Ellis Island. The German immigrants assimilated quickly early on, leading to the construction of German banks, insurance companies, and newspapers like the Baltimore Wecker, founded by Charles Henry Schnauffer. They're also, of course, responsible for the creation of the Berger Cookie, a Baltimore can't-live-without. By the late nineteenth century, most of the Germans coming over were German Jews, credited with the creation of most

Jewish institutions throughout the city, including Yiddish theaters like Concordia Hall, and synagogues like Eutaw Place Temple.

Also escaping war-torn Europe, the first Polish immigrants in Baltimore arrived in the mid 1860s in Fells Point, a majority of them running from the impending force of the Franco-Prussian War. Unlike the Germans, who took charge of the city, these Polish immigrants were unskilled workers from the countryside. As Baltimore, despite its border state location, was unapologetically pro-slavery, plantation owners turned to the Poles for cheap, easy labor after abolition. For years, the Polish were synonymous with the working class.

The twentieth century brought more war, and more immigrants. By 1914, the city's population was twenty percent German, and most public schools were known as German-English schools. World War II brought another 3,000 immigrants from Germany; however, the community was becoming more English driven. Russians also began widespread immigration to Baltimore in the early twentieth century, making Russians the largest foreign-born group in Baltimore in 1930. Most of these Russians, however, were extremely poor, and lived in slums together, separate from the assimilated Germans.

This culmination of cultures infused Baltimore with a perspective on the arts, music in particular. The second oldest singing society in the United States was the Baltimore Liederkranz, a German group formed in 1836. When Herr Wohlseiffer founded the society, he had no idea how big it would become. But in 1902, the group welcomed Prince Henry to Baltimore, cementing its spot in the books.

At the start of the 20th century, ragtime brought African American roots to light, and composers like Eubie Blake churned out some of the most striking tunes in American music. On Pennsylvania Avenue, jazz pulsed and bloomed. The Tijuana club was crowded with then little-known stars like Billie Holiday and Miles Davis. The intimate Le Coq d'Or hosted the famous Fuzzy Kane Trio whenever they stopped by. In this world, everyone in Baltimore was an immigrant, but the music always made it pretty easy to find home.

Psychedelic Baltimore

"We got to get ourselves back to the garden."

~"Woodstock," Crosby, Stills, Nash, and Young

Though almost 300 miles away, the Baltimorean crowd made it to Woodstock, New York, along with 300,000 other young people ready for change. Some made it by car, others by train, and some by a distinctive Volkswagen 1963 Model Year Kombi, decked out with colorful patterns and vibrant designs, each with its own in-depth symbolism, presenting itself as so much more than just a piece of psychedelic art, but also a definition for a generation. That was Bob Hieronimus' bus, and although he never made it to Woodstock, he left his own lasting impression on the historic music festival.

When asking around about the music scene around Baltimore, it's likely the name Bob Hieronimus will show up more than once (or twice). Artist, author, eccentric, and radio host, Hieronimus was a hippie before the word was coined. In college, he wore his hair long and dressed in cowboy boots, a few years early for the still innocent 1961. By the late 1960s, Hieronimus started work as an album cover designer for Elektra Records, but didn't end up finishing with the company. "I was auditioned to [design records], and courted by "the suits," but, as you know, my artwork is very intricate and deeply researched so that the symbols tell a story and the designs are all interlocking. It would take me six months to complete an album cover design, and when I found out they were offering me only $200 per album, I realized I would never make a living doing this," says Hieronimus.

Before he left the business, his interest in esoterica, astronomy, and the occult was a major selling point among musicians. His early work included promotional posters for Frank Zappa and the Lovin' Spoonful when they were in Baltimore. The posters attracted the attention of John Fred and His Playboy Band, known for their hit, "Judy in Disguise With Glasses" (they weren't exactly the Beatles). "They liked the style of my artwork, and appreciated that it taught lessons about the ageless wisdom teachings. The band members wanted to change their image and appear more serious than their bubblegum style. They gave me a referral to their manager in New York and told me to meet with him about designing their next album cover. This was the Summer of 1967. I met with the suits in New York and they confided in me that John Fred was a 'one hit wonder' and they didn't want me to waste my talents on a band that was already over. Instead they sent me to The Scene nightclub to meet Jimi Hendrix and other artists they thought I would connect with."

Out of all the musicians Hieronimus spent time with, Hendrix was the one he connected with most. "I was mostly impressed with how kind, gentle, and genuinely intelligent he was . . . I had always hoped that the inspiring words and stories in the songs of my favorite artists, such as the Beatles, Bob Dylan, Crosby Stills and Nash, etc. were truly felt and understood by the artists. Hendrix was indeed conscious of the meanings of his songs."

But by 1969, tired of the backstage scene, he was back, knees deep in a 2,700 square foot mural at Johns Hopkins University. On the side, he began painting cars, coating them in symbolic fixtures from hood to bumper, every color necessary. "I viewed painting vehicles as a way of creating mobile billboards that communicated ideas about the nature of existence and man's place in the universal scheme of things," says Hieronimus.

"Light," the legendary Woodstock bus, was named after a local Baltimore band fronted by Bob Grimm, who was friends with Hieronimus. The group drove the bus all the way up the New Jersey turnpike, only to be stopped right before the Woodstock festival entrance. Grimm remembers lying, "We're taking this bus to the art exhibit," to which the police replied "Okay, go ahead," setting an undeniable precedent for the positive energy and, more specifically, good fortune surrounding the "Light" bus.

Hieronimus was meticulous in his painting work, each color related to a specific trait. For example, white is tied to honor and purity, while blue is "religious inspiration." The detailed eagle and sphinx on each side door also carry ideas of wisdom, rebirth, and spirituality. "The story shown tells of advanced beings in the universe in various dimensions who are enabling and assisting our awareness and evolution to cosmic consciousness," he explains. Hieronimus was also influenced by the idea of the Aquarius Age, which is a part of imagery depicted on the bus.

Throughout the three day event, several musicians peeked inside the bus for a short while, and a Rolling Stone photographer caught the sensational shot of several Light band members lounging on the roof. Each photograph of the bus at Woodstock is yellow tinted and hazy, but coated in a blissed-out glory that can only be described as otherworldly peaceful.

Looking back, it's difficult to pinpoint whether the positive energy surrounding the bus determined its influence, or if Hieronimus' symbolism fueled the atmosphere instead. "The symbols I painted on this bus were very much in harmony with this powerful event Woodstock. It carried the message of who we are . . . Woodstock summed up the mood and feeling of a generation who could dream about peace and love in actuality." It's clear that somewhere along the New Jersey turnpike, a new generation had taken control. "The historical significance of the event at the time seemed to be the birth of a new spirit," Grimm wrote about his experience at Woodstock.

A group of young people that could take on the world was the general consensus of most festival-goers. Alan Fink, a Baltimore native and resident, went to Woodstock more on a whim than anything, taking up an offer from his roommate. Torrential downpour, mud, and food shortages are all accurate descriptions of the concert. What stands out most for Fink, though, is the solidarity of the movement as a whole.

In 1968, Fink and his roommates moved to Lincoln Park, "a major hippie hangout." There, he witnessed the trial of the Chicago 7, the shooting of Fred Hampton (leader of the Black Panthers), and the Democratic Convention riots. But the dark tone of grief in a splintering America was giving way to a beautiful power awakening in the young and the spirited.

This power came in several forms. One of them, Fink remembers vividly, "[I was] on the "L," which was jam packed with all of us boomers, all wearing black armbands, on our way downtown to demonstrate the deaths of the students at Kent State. I see that scene in the train to this day like a black and white documentary photograph etched into my brain . . . the sound of the train, the armbands, and most of all the quiet and somber faces of everyone."

The other form is more similar to Hieronimus' colorful Volkswagen bus, the idea that there is power in art and music. When Fink attended an anti-war protest at the Chicago Civic Center around 1969, he was struck mostly by the Chicago cast of "Hair," the controversial rock musical, performing "Aquarius" and "Let the Sunshine In" on top of the large Picasso sculpture in the center of the plaza. The lyrics of the songs reflect a world of idealism, a cure for the country:

Harmony and understanding
Sympathy and trust abounding
No more falsehoods or derisions
Golden living dreams of visions
Mystic crystal revelation
And the mind's true liberation

This solidarity in the awakening of the soul relates to Hieronimus' hidden message within the "Light" bus. When all sides of the bus are combined, Hieronimus explains the ultimate goal for America is revealed: "We Are All Earth People." Everyone at Woodstock must have understood, because when the bus returned to Baltimore, Hieronimus noticed the message concertgoers spray-painted on the side: "We are one."

Baltimore Remembers: What Was Your First Concert?

Photo by Melissa Peters

KISS in Philadelphia. It was March 24, 1976. It was my birthday present. My friend Lori and I were taken there by her older brother, Scott. I was thirteen and Lori was twelve. It was loud and crazy and I don't think we sat down through the entire show. They came back out and they played "Rock and Roll All Night," the people singing so loud you couldn't hear the band. My ears rang for days.

~Sharon Dobson

The Go Go's. Seventh grade. Our parents dropped us off at the arena and picked us up later!

~Missie DeCelle Wilcox

Shaun Cassidy. It was at the Civic Center and I went with my parents and brother. I remember he split his pants and ran off stage. He came back on stage wearing an Orioles jersey, and I'm guessing a new pair of pants.

~Linda Lampel Esterson

Fleetwood Mac—my older brother took me. I was probably about ten years old.

~Michelle Rosen Heyman

Sonny and Cher at the Civic Center. Went from Silver Spring with my high school boyfriend.

~Arlene Nagel Bekman

STYX, maybe 1977, at the Civic Center in Baltimore with the boy across the street.

~Ann Holden Harris

Senior year in high school—Beach Boys and Jim Croce at Carnegie Hall with Maddy Hall, my [best friend] in junior high. Concert date was November 23, 1972. It would have been for Maddy's birthday, which was the 22nd. Tickets were $5.50. We had seats in the "nosebleed" section.

~Toni Greenberg

1980, The Cars at Merriweather—lawn seats. Went with my boyfriend. Can't remember the ticket price, but it couldn't have been too much since my [boyfriend] worked at Roy Rogers and didn't have a lot of money.

~Alice Stochl Perez

Sha Na Na. Went with my parents to see them at the Painter's Mill Music Hall somewhere around 1979 or 1980. After that I know I saw Bryan Adams in 1984 at Merriwether. I also vividly remember seeing Bruce Springsteen at RFK [Stadium] for the Born to Run tour in 1984, and remember we bought our nosebleed seats for $70, which was pretty expensive for 1984.

~Lisa Sparks

Golden Earring and Patty Smyth at Painter's Mill Theater.

~Lisa Fidler Yarmis

America at the long gone Capital Centre. It was so disappointing—they might as well have been playing a record!

~Nancy M. Jackson

Van Halen, September 1979 in Corpus Christi, Texas. My sister, Terri, took me along with her friend, Sharon, who literally screamed during the concert that David Lee Roth was singing directly to her. That might have been true. We were only eight rows back and she was sitting on some dude's shoulders.

~Richard Train

Donny and Marie at Merriweather. They couldn't sell the tickets so they gave free ones to my Brownie troop.

~Erica Siegel Hobby

Journey, August 1981, Columbia, MD, Merriweather Post Pavilion. Escape tour. I didn't know the people who took me. It was an extra ticket they had to sell. I think it was $15. Crammed on the hump seat in the back of a Granada, we drove 60 minutes from Dundalk to Columbia. That sucked. I wasn't overly excited since I had never been to any kind of live show. I was fifteen years old. I had not heard Journey on the radio much yet. To my amazement, these people who I just met had fourth row seats. I was still wondering what the big deal was. That is, until Steve Perry started singing ... When he sang ... I was stunned. That man was amazing. They rocked us right out of there, exhausted. That night is when I truly started to understand rock 'n' roll and to love music.

~Tom Sinor

Foreigner, 1978, Capital Centre. Don't remember the price, but we all got high from second hand pot smoke.

~Janine Framm

My first Baltimore concert was Emerson, Lake, and Palmer at the Civic Center . . . in the late 70s . . . I will never forget Keith Emerson flipping over his organ while playing it. It was on top of him at one point. Amazing.

~Mitch Dickler

Huey Lewis and the News! Merriweather. Freshman year of college. [Approximately] $20.

~Michael Schuman

My first concert was a date and he took me to see Bread. Must have been around 1972 and either at UM or Constitution Hall.

~Peggy Hennessey Scherr

Dr. Hook with Joe Cocker at Mechanics Hall in Worcester with Rita Ernenwein-Williams when we were in junior high.

~Tracy Donham Smith

Couldn't get to see the Beatles, so we went to see Dave Clark Five. Probably in early high school in D.C. Went with a girlfriend. Screamed all night! Enjoyed it, but the crowd was a bit overwhelming.

~Beverly Barnhard

Elton John, August 1976, outdoors at Rich Stadium in suburban Buffalo, New York. [With] some other friends I was going to college with at the time. It was about $20 per person. It rained a lot.

~David Rothenberg

Herman's Hermits at the Steel Pier in Atlantic City—1966.

~Steve Ehrenpreis

Badfinger at Calvert Hall (High School) was my first concert. It was in 1973. I was a Loyola High junior at the time. I wore one of my father's sports coats, as many preppies did back then. I climbed one of the walls to stand in an elevated window sill until security kicked me off. My future (and present) wife said she remembered seeing me confronted by security. As we didn't formally meet until four years later, it's hard to validate her memory!

~Dan Schuman

Jefferson Airplane, Stony Brook University, 1970.

~Lola Hahn

The Police at the [Capital] Centre with my brother, Kevin. I think the tickets were, like, $10 or something? I remember that because of a snowstorm they did not hang speakers from the ceiling for the show.

~Brian Shea

Paul McCartney and Wings, Capital Centre in 1976 or 1977. About ten of us stayed overnight at a friend's house. We didn't have advance tickets and I don't recall the price. We waited eight hours in the rain, under taps, listening to guitarists playing Beatles songs. It was amazing. When they let us in, people *stormed* in. I was standing two rows from the stage. People pushed toward the stage so hard my feet were about a foot off the ground.

~Beth Sheely

Loverboy, City Island, Harrisburg, PA. Can't remember if we had tickets or if we just watched and listened from the other side of the fence.

~Lisa Lessick Dickler

I saw Crack the Sky two or three times at Painter's Mill in 1980/81. But my first big show was Ozzy Osbourne (with Def Leppard opening) at Merriweather on August 6, 1981. Row J, seat 105, center section. My seat cost $11. That was still the loudest show I've ever been to . . . my ears rang for two days afterwards!

~Joel Hammerman

Raised on the Radio

"That was the big thing when I was growing up, singing on the radio. The extent of my dream was to sing on the radio station in Memphis. Even when I got out of the Air Force in 1954, I came right back to Memphis and started knocking on doors at the radio station."

~Johnny Cash

The thing about the music is that it was easy to miss if you weren't careful. Without modern day delicacies like search engines, good music meant catching the right radio programs at the right moment, scouting for the good record stores, finding the people who knew a little something about something else. It was a thrilling hunt and in some ways, luck of the draw. A flip of the dial could mean the next big thing if a band or musician had played their cards right.

Radio, in particular, capitalized in knowing its listeners. Small, independent stations played what the listeners wanted, and what the listeners didn't even know they wanted, snatching up then-obscure groups that were still foreign to mostly everyone else. From Baltimore to the D.C. area, WHFS was legendary. "They were the progressive station at a time when what you heard on the radio was controlled by music directors," says music promoter Tom Carrico. "[WHFS] had pretty much total freedom to play whatever they wanted." The station was transformed from a low-rating, easy-listening station to a Baltimore/D.C. icon in 1969, all because of three semi-out-there, but completely music-driven Bard College graduates, Sara Vass, Mark Gorbulew, and Joshua Brooks.

WHFS grew hot fast and was soon responsible for "mainstreaming" some of the most influential musicians of its time. "They were essential in supporting and developing the early careers of Bruce Springsteen and Little Feat," explains Carrico. Springsteen's first two albums, *Greetings from Asbury Park, N. J.* and *The Wild, the Innocent & the E Street Shuffle*, spread his early, more jazz-based sound mainly through radio. WHFS was one the first to catch on.

And still, between the Springsteen and Bonnie Raitt, the station played plenty of local bands that quickly reached the same household name status in Baltimore as the international bands. Carrico managed the Nighthawks, a high-energy blues band from D. C., who became a favorite on WHFS.

At the time, radio was also taking on an educational stance. Music education, of course. Rock 'n' roll is never simply rock 'n' roll, and WHFS recognized that, branching out beyond the expected contemporary music. The station included jazz, folk, blues, even zydeco in its setlists. Duke Ellington sometimes followed a modern blues act, or maybe a Frank Zappa ditty—and it worked.

Rock 'n' roll on the radio was exciting, vibrant, intense. The disc jockeys' booming personalities were like a whole other music genre wedged in between the songs. They were the good guys, among the few adults who spoke teenagers' language. They gave them the music and defended it against the enemy with an iron shield. They used their powerful platforms for good. Alan Freed, likely the most renowned and controversial DJ in rock history, not only preached respect for the music, but undoubtedly loved it just as much as his listeners. He once declared, "Anyone who says rock 'n' roll is a passing fad or a flash-in-the-pan trend along the music road has *rocks in the head*, dad!"

Of course, Freed's influence extended pretty far beyond the music. His enthusiastic and often unfiltered on-air discussions regarding the blues he played led to tense conversations on the relationship between racial segregation and radio. Now, Freed wasn't the only DJ out there playing "black" music, but he was one of the few broadcasting it to a young, and generally white audience. On WJW in Cleveland, where Freed worked, he was decades ahead of his time, and despite his popularity, plenty of folk were turned off by such a progressive approach to radio.

Before the Top 40 format was introduced, most of these independent stations and DJs played their own personal favorite records, or new bands that they themselves loved. As rock 'n' roll slowly inched itself toward corporate, love for the music communicated *by* music lovers and *to* music lovers was an increasingly rare phenomenon.

And because these DJs and stations were doing the dirty work, digging out the underground groups and singers and thrusting them into the mainstream, music as a whole was able to transition. Alan Freed gave blues a doorway to wider audiences, which in turn, persuaded young kids across the nation and the ocean to start picking up guitars for the first time, which resulted in blues-inspired music—also known as rock 'n' roll. Radio was, more than anything, a device for communication, and the message of music just as valued as the news broadcasts.

Johnny Dark

Johnny Dark turned radio into a force of nature in Baltimore during the 50s and 60s. As rock 'n' roll was just starting to find its voice, Dark created an epicenter for the music through the WCAO station, honing in a ratings share of 68.3.

With Dark, the music was given a place to stay and a chance. He not only snatched it up off the street, but also dusted it off and presented it as worthwhile. By the mid-1960s, labels in music felt less necessary than they had in the 50s. Rock 'n' roll was no longer black and white, rather, a thousand different shades ranging from Stevie Wonder to The Doors to Aretha Franklin to Bob Dylan. Dark pulled from all genres and backgrounds, breaking subtle walls most listeners weren't even aware existed. His catchphrase, "You heard it here first on WCAO" was usually true.

Despite his local legacy, Dark wasn't native to Baltimore. Born Albert Bennett, Dark grew up in Cambridge, Massachusetts. By 1953, he was already scoping out Cambridge for jobs in radio, but was forced to complete his military service first. This was no problem for Dark, who became a disc jockey and announcer at Fort Belvoir, Virginia for several years, gaining plenty of experience for a program of his own. He eventually worked his way up to WCAO-AM in 1961. His radio name, "Johnny Dark," was a suggestion from a friend who enjoyed the 1954 Tony Curtis movie.

Most remember Dark as professional and dedicated, as well as easygoing and humble. Dark was once told the Baltimore Sun, he felt he had "never worked a day in his life." And it was pretty obvious why. Dark spent time at several local venues and functions along with his radio broadcasts, providing background broadcasts to different events throughout the years. These events ranged from nudist colony dances in Crownsville to interviews with George Harrison.

Dark's familiar voice was immortalized in the 1988 record, *Cruisin'*, which captured a 1968 WCAO broadcast in full form. The record includes "Magic Carpet Ride" by Steppenwolf, "Midnight Confessions" by The Grass Roots, and "Love Child" by Marvin Gaye. Original commercials and promotions from the broadcast still appear, a peppy Doublemint Gum commercial wedged in between The Box Tops and The Temptations, naturally.

One of the first disc jockeys to show excitement and extensive knowledge concerning the music, Dark's style set the precedent for most programs that followed. Dark passed away September of 2016 at 82 years old.

Do You Remember Rock 'N' Roll Radio

WCVT

During the 1970s and 1980s, Towson University's college run radio station, WCVT, had a major fan base. The station first signed on air with Jack Freeberger in 1971 as WVTS and only reached as far as the Student Union building on campus. In 1975, the station switched to WCVT. Radio personality, Babs Levedahl was the first to utter the new name on air. The station was largely alternative and run completely through students. It was the sort of station people tuned into for a familiar voice, a favorite show. Listeners memorized the station schedule, and were comforted in knowing that twenty-one hours a day, WCVT would be there, at the ready.

WCVT Disc Jockeys 1980

Brice Freeman	Larry Steinbeck	Snoopy Crowder
Kevin Estis	Kimberly Laxton	Jerry Toulas
Debbie White	Jeff Dugan	Babs Levedahl
Paul DePasquale	Jim Carter	Bill Logan
Spiro Morakas	John Johnson	Bruce Eller
Roberta Cowan	Rod Misey	Tim Dawson

WCVT Album Playlist September 1989

1. Ed's Redeeming Qualities – *Ed's Day*
2. Ramones – *Brain Dead*
3. Tin Machine – *UT*
4. Mary My Hope – *Museum*
5. Pixies – *Doolittle*
6. The Cost of Living – *Comic Book Page*
7. Lemonheads – *Lick*
8. Dead Milkmen – *Smokin' Banana Peels*
9. 24-7 Spyz – *Harder Than You*
10. Tom Tom Club – *Boom Boom Chi Boom*

WLPL

For most of the 1960s, WLPL was known as WSID. In 1969, the station dedicated itself to pure album rock, playing mainly 45 RPM vinyl singles. About a year later, the station adopted WLPL, 'LPL' in place for "Land of Pleasant Listening." From there, the music was a compilation of Top 40 hits.

WLPL Disc Jockeys

Joe Pachino
Chuck Weaver

WLPL Top 10 Hits from the Week of January 12, 1975

1. Elton John – "Lucy in the Sky With Diamonds"
2. Eagles – "Best Of My Love"
3. Carpenters – "Please Mr. Postman"
4. Barry Manilow – "Mandy"
5. Jethro Tull – "Bungle in the Jungle"
6. Doobie Brothers – "Black Water"
7. Barry White – "You're The First"
8. Gloria Gaynor – "Never Can Say Goodbye"
9. Paul Anka – "One Man Woman/One Woman Man"
10. Elvis Presley – "Promised Land"

WKTK

WKTK was a progressive rock station, the first station in the Baltimore area to broadcast and operate with quadrasonic sound. A quadrasonic sound system uses four channels for speakers instead of one, producing signals that are, in large part, completely independent of one another. The station was operated under Carl Brenner, who encouraged broadcasting live rock performances in front of large audiences. On January 22, 1971, the station spent the day at the Baltimore Civic Center during a youth exposition. A total of ten bands performed, along with several folk and jazz groups. WKTK also released LPs during its time on the air.

WTKT - Baltimore's Best Rock 1978 LP Track List

1. Taurus – "Traveler"
2. Basement Floor – "Hideaway"
3. Both Worlds – "Fish Bait"
4. Kashmir – "Texas City"
5. Danon Wright – "Down and Out"
6. Appaloosa – "All Night My Friend'
7. Hollins Ferry – "Turn Your Back"
8. Oho – "Seldom Bought"
9. Springwood – "For the Land"
10. John Seay/Alan Dawson – "One Way Ticket"
11. Climbadonkey – "Golden Throat"

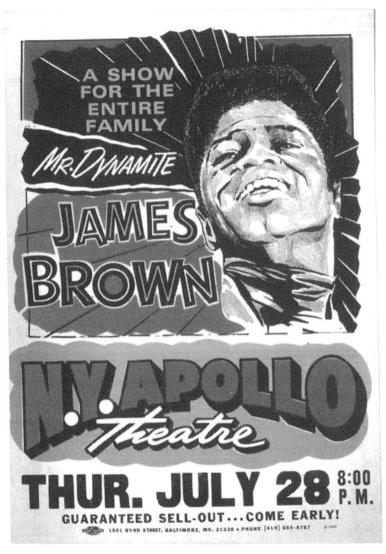

Globe Collection and Press at MICA

Communication Breakdown

"Don't try to explain it, just sell it."

~Colonel Tom Parker, Elvis Presley's manager

For a company that holds a significant portion of Baltimore music history, Globe Poster's beginnings were a bit unconventional. Really, it all started over a card game in Philadelphia in 1929. When Harry Shapiro, a printer hailing from Texas, proposed going into business with the well-to-do Norman Goldstein from New York, Goldstein couldn't refuse. The question of where they would locate their new business was quickly answered by opening a map of the East Coast and folding it, the crease landing smack on Baltimore. It must have been fate because the next eighty or so years turned Baltimore's finest poster-printing business into a landmark.

The first posters Globe printed advertised mostly carnivals, burlesque houses, and films, which helped to keep the new business afloat amidst the fast-striking Great Depression. "It's a poor man's advertising," Bob Cicero once said. Cicero's father, Joseph Cicero Sr. had purchased the business from Norman Shapiro (Harry's brother) in 1975.

Baltimore, a working class city, fell quickly into the desperation of the Depression era. Unemployed men and women sold apples on street corners. Mile long lines stretched across the city as people waited for daily bread. Films were escapist and indulgent. And the posters were nothing if not efficient, driving people to spend their money for just a few hours of the blissfully unaware Cary Grant, a familiar face removed from what had become a regularly miserable reality.

By the time Norman Shapiro took over the business from his brother in 1954, changes came about in the form of poster subject. After the Depression, big band music gained momentum in the business. Early Globe posters promoted Glenn Miller, Duke Ellington, the Dorsey Brothers, Bing and Bobby Crosby, Billie Holiday. And, then, just a couple decades later, music started bending genres, breaking barriers, quickly becoming Globe's priority.

Blown up prints advertising musicians like Etta James, B.B, King, and James Brown spread out across the nation, ranging from soul to jazz, from blues to the first strums of what would become rock 'n' roll. These posters were groundbreaking in that they validated black musicians. Suddenly, this was a show you didn't want miss. This was music worth your time. And with the names of the music acts printed in impossibly fat lettering at the top of the poster, or in long, slender lines down the middle, it was hard to miss the excitement and appeal the poster advertised.

This was mostly thanks to Harry Knorr, who spent three decades with Globe polishing its distinct style. The early posters used basswood letterpressing, with specific cuts designed for more commonly used words like "the" and "and." Around the mid-1950s, Knorr introduced Day-Glo ink to Globe, a cheaper ink option made of fish scales that, while didn't *literally* glow, allowed for a wide range of vivid, neon hues the printers could stripe against the poster background. Bob Cicero explains, "Against the landscape of trees, roads, brick and concrete, fluorescent colors stand out. They catch your eye and can't be missed. When a street light or a car headlight hits the color they illuminate." In other words, the posters worked. Knorr once said, "If you can't read a poster in three seconds or less, it isn't a successful poster."

Globe posters are credited with creating and producing the visual aesthetic for an entire era of musicians. Most of Globe's workers weren't artists themselves. The workers consisted mainly of working class guys from around

Baltimore. What they may not have known then was that the visual history of their poster-making helped to define the music groups and singers of the era.

Most of these young black musicians couldn't afford radio advertisements, and word-of-mouth was tricky business. The Globe posters were their main-line for communication, and, ultimately, for getting the name out there. Solomon Burke and Otis Redding, Muddy Waters and LaVern Baker, names we know because Globe gave them a foothold in mainstream culture. Globe introduced us first. Along with sound, these musicians are remembered for their splashy posters that color-coated city streets, pieces of Baltimore spread out across the nation.

TAVERN OWNERS N.U.L.D.A.
PRESENTS THE 10th ANNUAL
SCHOLARSHIP DANCE
FEATURING

SAM *and* DAVE

AND THEIR
ORCHESTRA

SOLOMON BURKE

ROBERT TREAT HOTEL
MAIN BALLROOM
— 50 PARK PLACE -- NEWARK, N. J. —

SUN. APR. 27

9:00 P.M.
'till
1:00 A.M.

ADVANCE ADMISSION $10.00 -- AT DOOR $12.00
FOR RESERVATIONS CALL...
(201) 678-2885 • 623-5123 • 485-9897 • 248-8127

123 Market Place • Baltimore, Md. 21202 • Ph. (301) 685-8787

Globe Collection and Press at MICA

Couldn't Get a Ticket (It Was a Sold Out Show)

"I have never experienced anything like walking out onto the stage of an oversold venue and, before the first note is struck, realizing that there is not going to be enough oxygen for all of us."

~Henry Rollins

Music promoter Tom Carrico describes Baltimore as a "breathing city": A city where the music not only pulses, but thrives, where vibe is key, where every club, and every pub, is a familiar face and a familiar name. Around the city, music acts that passed through Baltimore or found their start here were introduced to the area through underground taverns and hangouts, places made by locals and for locals. These venues stood as a direct link between the people and the music, little corners of a decidedly blue collar city where blues, jazz, swing, and later rock and roll could entirely transform the atmosphere, if just for one gig.

On Eutaw Street, No Fish Today was a dive bar, its name most ironic for a port city. After opening in 1969, it featured $3 beers, and raw talent every week. Stevie Ray Vaughan and Double Trouble was one of those acts. Carrico managed to book three different Mid-Atlantic tours for Vaughan, and at every stop in Baltimore, No Fish Today was the place to be. The bar stayed afloat through the resurgence of 1970s blues, found mostly in Vaughan's act, and in other passing bands like the Nighthawks and blues revisionist, Billy Price.

Just around the corner from No Fish Today, The Old Marble Bar found its niche as an alternative nightclub. Formed by musicians LesLee and Roger Anderson in 1978, the club served as a gathering center for proto-punk and art rock, predecessors to the up-and-coming punk movement. Nationally recognized bands like REM and icons like Iggy Pop made a name for themselves early in their careers when passing through Baltimore. Carrico booked several Nighthawk shows at The Old Marble Bar when he managed the band in the late 70s. "I remember walking over there on a very hot August night. Root Boy Slim and the Sex Change Band were playing. It was so hot, one of the godawful humid days we get in August. As I walked down the very few stairs from the sidewalk to the club entrance, I felt a little bit of warmth. I opened the door and the heat inside the club, just from all the people being inside, almost knocked me off my feet," Carrico laughs.

The Old Marble Bar was in the basement of the Congress Hotel on West Franklin Street. Just one level below, old catacombs tucked behind a secret passageway, along with large Roman baths unused for decades. The upper levels of The Congress Hotel tell a different story. Along with the Old Marble Bar, the hotel hosted the Baltimore Pub. (Legend has it that both F. Scott Fitzgerald and Humphrey Bogart frequented the bar.) The pub consisted of one small room. Carrico worked shows with Bart Hackner, who ran the pub at the time, searching out talents like NRBQ, a multi-genre band ranging from rock to jazz, known for high-energy performances, and an a capella group, The Persuasions.

At some point in the 70s, Carrico booked the Nighthawks at the Famous Ballroom. He remembers it fondly as "one of the finest venues for blues, jazz, swing, any kind of roots music, particularly if it's danceable." The Left Bank Jazz Society booked most of the performances, and Sunday jazz matinees brought in plenty of profit. Located on Charles Street, on the same block as the Charles Theater, the Famous Ballroom invented the idea of vibe in Baltimore. On the back wall hung framed black and white photos of jazz gurus who played there, including Miles Davis and John Coltrane. Some even believe the Famous Ballroom is where Coltrane played his last show ever.

On the ceiling, paintings of stars and planets circled around each other. "The vibe of the place was like you were going back in time to the 40s or 50s, like an old honky tonk, but on a much larger scale," says Carrico, giving new meaning to the Rolling Stones' "Honky Tonk Woman." The room was grand, and could fit up to eight hundred people at a time. The venue was also B. Y. O. B. Hundreds of show-goers brought their own drinks carried in flimsy paper bags. The ballroom sold set-ups for the drinks, where people made money from what they brought.

While jazz was integral to the Famous Ballroom, the subgenres that started popping up in the late 60s and early 70s integrated into the setlists with ease. George Thorogood performed at the Ballroom during his touring, as well as Stevie Ray Vaughan. Vaughan had passed through Baltimore often during his run at No Fish Today. By the time he made it to the Famous Ballroom, his concert was sold-out, which was lucky for the Baltimore Blues Society, the beneficiary of the charity concert.

By the 1960s, most of these venues were considered for "older" generations, which really just meant people over 30. Despite the blues' inherent connection to rock and roll, most kids still considered it their parents' music, music that commemorated the pain of the past, and all the Jim Crow, old south wrapped up in it. Things were complicated. Suddenly white people liked black music, and vice versa. As barriers were broken down one by one, it was difficult for kids to find their own personal connection to it all. In Baltimore, The Famous Ballroom was tasteful, but too old school. No Fish Today was popular, but also more or less beaten down. In response, the new trend of discotheques sparked around the city. Some places were more intimate, others much larger, packed tightly, where young people came to listen to records and dance. The scenes were casual, fun, the experience of the place just as valuable as the music it played. By the mid-1960s, almost a dozen discotheques opened in Baltimore. Of course, teenage fads live and die in a matter of seconds, and by 1967, most of these places were already bored and shutting down. The Bluesette on North Charles Street, was the only survivor.

An article that ran in the Baltimore Magazine in 1967 credits the owner, Arthur Peyton, for keeping the teen center up and running. "He is the embodiment of the youth movement, and all that it involves, freak outs, be-ins, happenings. He has not lost contact and, consequently, youth accepts him," Eirik Tecumseh Blom explained in the piece. Peyton seemed to understand what the kids valued in music. The "total environment" of the place, as Peyton said, was Haight-Ashbury, young musicians playing mainly Jefferson Airplane, The Seeds, Oedipus and the Mothers. And the best part? No parents allowed. Baltimore wasn't privy to its own Greenwich Village or Sunset Strip. And those places wouldn't have fit into Baltimore. This was private paradise for teens everyone knows, neighbors, friends. These kids weren't fancy; most regulars at the Bluesette hadn't been raised that way. This was a compilation of everyone who was simply looking for a place to go and be.

The main room of the Bluesette was almost entirely dark, save for a few lanterns. Photographs that survived the club are grainy and difficult to make out. Abstract paintings hung from the walls, although once the strobe lights turned on during a performance, it was nearly impossible to see anything at all. The amplifiers were at their maximum volume, the noise almost excruciating. Tightly wound crowds swayed and flailed. "Total environment," yes, and total experience, too. There was something about being there, surrounded by a hundred other kids your age, caught in the same trance of music. It was an island paradise where the kids ruled and the music reigned.

Caption and image by Stuart Zolotorow

"Mick Jagger, 1981. There had been a bomb scare right before the start of the show. I had made friends with the Stone's bodyguards—a very large African American called 'Tiny.' He told me there was a chance they may cancel. He also showed me a door under the stage that I could escape through as they expected a riot if the show was scrapped! The show went on without a hitch but delayed 1/2 hour. Song he is singing is "Start Me Up." As we were leaving the pit, Mick picked up a bucket of water and threw it on a couple of the photographers... I didn't get wet, as I was leaving the pit area. Apparently, he didn't like that they were staying in the pit longer than we were allowed to (first 3 songs is standard for photography). If you have a ticket, you can stay, but your cameras can't be with you."

The Other Artists

"We wanted revelations, and we got them."

~Jann Wenner, co-founder of Rolling Stone magazine

Walking into Stuart Zolotorow's photography studio is like visiting a museum. Before you enter, a large, framed portrait of Eric Clapton hangs framed in the stairwell. It's a recent picture, and Clapton definitely looks his age. Still, with the way he's holding his guitar—like a bucking horse he's trying to tame—there aren't many differences from similar shots forty years ago. Other framed pictures of The Rolling Stones, B.B. King, and Willie Nelson line the walls. Press passes, both cloth and paper, dangle from the corner of each frame, spotted with age and fading. If you squint, the year 1981 can just barely be made out on the press pass near B.B. King. Stuart explains that this concert was just two months after John Lennon was shot.

Farther into the studio, a Beatles shrine—"shrine" is the only word that could possibly describe the level of Beatles devotion present in this room— stretches across the room. A large photo of John Lennon and Yoko Ono, both wearing sunglasses, sits surrounded by original 1960s collectables: Beatles figurines, lunch boxes, dolls, posters, miniature yellow submarines. "I saved everything my parents ever got me in the 60s," Stuart says. And his collection kept growing. A pair of Ringo Starr drum sticks from several years ago sits neatly on a desk next to guitar picks from Paul McCartney, David Crosby, and Ziggy Marley. Moving through the shelves, brightly-colored Beatles statues morph into solitary Lennon figures. A heavy silver-colored one with a tiny Lennon sitting casually against a wall is made from melted down handguns. On the back, a note: the statue is number 139 out of 5,000.

Filing cabinets are off to the side, stuffed with Rolling Stone first editions and stacks of picture prints. On top of one cabinet is a speaker, the best of the Beatles filtering through with an electric, larger-than-life sound. As Stuart begins to speak, recalling and reliving the moments, the Beatles songs help tell his stories, changing colors with the mood of each anecdote. It's almost supernatural how "Here Comes the Sun" bursts into the room as he gets to the part where his photo made it to the cover of the magazine. Or how B.B. King's death seems to happen "While My Guitar Gently Weeps."

Without the photographers, journalists, filmmakers, and artists who chronicled the times, rock 'n' roll wouldn't be where it is today. Not even close. The music is a fluid, easy to pour out, and difficult to capture again. These storytellers have held stories in place throughout the decades, practically cementing the times. In 1968, the world saw the Monterey Pop Music Festival through the lens of filmmaker D.A. Panabaker. In this sense, Jim Morrison, Janis Joplin, Otis Redding became more than just their voices, faceless on a record. Personified—they became icons.

Journalism, too, has broken the strangely silent side of music. In 1976, "Good Vibrations" was finally unlayered, revealing a painful vulnerability. Brian Wilson explained to journalist David Felton in Rolling Stone magazine:

My mother used to tell me about vibrations. I didn't really understand too much of what that meant when I was a boy. It scared me, the word "vibrations." To think that invisible feelings, invisible vibrations existed, scared me to death. But she told me about dogs that would bark at people and then not bark at others, that a dog would pick up vibrations from these people that you can't see, but you can feel. And the same existed with people.

49

In a way, music will always be a gut reaction. It's when people around the music take a closer look that actual revelations will come about. The "other" artists fill in the blanks for what the rest of us can't see or wouldn't have known on our own.

Thanks for that, guys.

Image by Stuart Zolotorow

A Day in the Life with Photographer Stuart Zolotorow

"There were a lot of kids into rock and roll all over the place, but I was probably into it more than anybody."

When did you first discover photography?

In 1974, the thing I wanted to do was make film. I took film classes through school and animation classes in school. I was getting pretty good at it. Then I met this guy, Harding Roberts. Harding was a customer of ours. I worked at a place called Zeppe's Photo. Harding was very famous and had won two Academy Awards for a movie he made on the Nuremberg Trials.

Harding said [to me],

"You have a really good command for photography. I see for you making it faster in photography than in the film world."

And the one thing he said to me that kind of stuck was, "You have to be able to pay people to get you into the film industry. If I were you, I would go through the route of photography." So that's what I decided to do.

What was it about rock and roll that made you want to photograph it?

Well, I think everything in my life sort of centered around the music business. Because I absolutely loved rock and roll. And I knew I couldn't play well enough to make it as a musician.

When did you start playing guitar?

I started in 1968. And I still have my first guitar.

He grabs an old acoustic guitar leaning against a wall. There are chips in the wood around the soundhole, and two slightly faded signatures on the body.

This is an old fender guitar signed by Willie Nelson and B. B. King. I don't play it anymore because it's really kind of losing it a little bit. And I don't want to take it out. I used to take it everywhere before the guys signed it. But I stopped because I didn't want anything to happen to it.

[I started playing because] I just absolutely loved rock 'n' roll. I was hooked. And I was one of those kids in 1964 who saw The Beatles on the Ed Sullivan Show. My neighbors were over and all the neighbors were watching it on our TV. They all said, 'My kids will never have long hair like they have!' But I was hooked.

Was there a disconnect between you and your parents—the older generation?

I was very lucky. My father was a magazine publisher. In the late 1960s, the company that he worked for bought Rolling Stone magazine. They got the publishing rights for it. Anything in the first year of Rolling Stone magazine was just printed in San Francisco on very dingy, raggy paper. I remember my dad coming into my room saying, "My company just got the rights to work for the publishers for Rolling Stone magazine." And he showed me the first issue, which was what they considered back then a 'back issue'.

It had a picture of John Lennon on the front wearing an army helmet because John was making a movie called How I Won the War. *It was the first thing that he did—that any of [the Beatles] did—by himself without the other three. And I remember taking that magazine and I remember cutting out the picture of John and taping it to my wall. Well, now that magazine . . . you can buy reprints of it for $150. To get an original one—I've only seen one once in person at the Newseum—to buy one of those right now, it's several thousand dollars.*

When Rolling Stone first came out, it was a real cheap paper. None of the magazine stores wanted to carry because it didn't fit in with the rest of the magazines. So my dad took me during during the week—during the summer—to work with him. And he took me to the main offices of Giant Food, which was near D.C. And we went inside. My dad's wearing a suit and I'm wearing, you know, a shirt and bell bottoms.

He took me inside and I remember the guy he met with, his name was Izzy. And my father was on really good terms with this guy. And he said,

"Bernie [Stuart's father], what I am I going to do with this thing? Nobody's going to buy this thing."

And my father said, "Yes, they will." He was a really gruff guy, this Izzy guy.

And I remember him turning to me, and he said, "What do you think of this?"

I said, "Well, it's got the Beatles on the cover, it's going to sell."

He said, "For '----'s sake, Bernie, I'll try it."

So for my father to get a magazine into Giant Food, it was a big deal. At that point, Giant was the biggest supermarket of its kind. And then any time he had tried to sell the magazine into another store, he would say, "Well, I got it into Giant Food." And then the drug stores would let them.

He would take me back to check the different stores, and they weren't putting it out. They were getting the magazines in the stores, and they were tearing off the covers. When you work in the magazine business, to get credits for magazines that don't sell, you just tear off the cover and send that back to the publisher to get credit for it. The rest of the magazine just gets shredded. The magazines were already torn when we were getting there. So my dad came up with a special kind of holder to put the magazines in. He would take them to the stores and make sure Rolling Stone was front and center. He did that for as long as I can remember.

My mom, she was really cool, too. My mom used to go to the Hippodrome Theater. The equivalent to the people that I love, the people of those days was Sinatra. My mom used to go for a quarter see Sinatra sing and then watch a movie.

Last year I photographed Crosby, Stills, and Nash at the Hippodrome and after the show I went backstage and I was talking to Graham. I told him this was a really historic theater and how my mom used to come here and see Sinatra for a quarter.

And then one time she went and she decided to watch both shows for the same quarter. (Laughs) And my grandfather wouldn't let her go back to see Sinatra anymore. And it *wasn't until my wife, Karen and I, took her to see Sinatra that she got actually see him again after fifty years.*

My folks were cool. In 1977, my mom knew that I wanted to meet John Lennon, so my dad, working through Rolling Stone, found out where John Lived. My mom took me and we got on a train, and we went to the apartment in New York. My mom, she just walked into the apartment. And Yoko came out in the hallway and [my mom] said, you know, "My son wants to meet John." And Yoko's wearing this huge fur coat. Hold on, I got a photo of it.

Stuart gets up to look through a nearby cabinet, lifting stack after stack of magazines and photographs. He pulls out a large frame. Inside are two tiny, yet distinct photographs of Yoko and John, Yoko's coat is dark brown and thick, bunched around her neck where her long hair draped down. Below the pictures are polaroid-sized squares with a fading signature on each.

This is in the hallway of their apartment.

He points to the picture where the side of his face is shown next to John.

That's me, in 1977, with my little beard. And my mom had fixed Yoko's hair and everything. Yoko said to my mom, "You know, everybody wants to meet my husband. And I just can't do it with everybody."

After we met her, we sent photos like this to her, and she and John both signed them.

What's involved in getting and completing an assignment from magazines like Rolling Stone?

Rolling Stone I've never been able to get into, which is crazy. I have sent photos to them over the years. I sent six really nice photos of Prince to them when Prince passed away. I've sent photos of John and Yoko to them. Last week I sent some new photos of McCartney to them, because they put McCartney on the cover of their latest issue.

Stuart goes over to his large filing cabinets and pulls out a stack of first edition *Rolling Stone* magazines, each one wrapped in a plastic cover. He holds up one.

This was the one year anniversary of Rolling Stone. Obviously, it's John and Yoko, and they're naked on the cover. John actually shot the photo himself, setting a tripod up.

He pulls out more.

*These are all from the 60s and 70s. And these letters here (*he points to the top corner of a magazine), *IND, that's 'Independent News Company,' the company my dad worked for. These here are even older; these are from 1967. The Beatles were on [the cover] four times, while they were still a group. Now you can't even find these.*

Caption and image by Stuart Zolotorow

"McCartney, December 1989. This was the first night of his first American tour since John Lennon's death (9 years since his last tour, 13 years since his last tour of the States). If he was nervous, we couldn't tell. I was shooting for the *Baltimore Sun,* it was actually used on the front page of the "Arts section" when he came to Washington in 1990. Apparently, Linda really liked the image, and I was invited backstage when they came to DC. The Song he was singing is "Figure of 8" from his new LP called "Flowers in the Dirt.""

He sifts through several magazine covers and holds up one of the four Beatles.

This is a shot that Linda McCartney took. This is probably one of the last photos of them ever taken together. It's on the November, 1969 issue of Rolling Stone.

So, yeah I've tried. I've tried to get the cover, to get something *on Rolling Stone and I've never been able to crack it.*

Stuart pulls out several magazines with cover photos he shot. He pulls out one with John and Yoko.

This is a magazine called The National Examiner. *And then this is my cover of Pete Townshend on a magazine I shoot for all the time called* Goldmine Magazine. *And then this is John and Yoko on the cover of* Goldmine. *But they flopped [the image].*

He holds up an image with John and Yoko standing on different sides.

See, this is the right way that it's supposed to be. They made it backward because they thought it would make the quotation work better. The whole thing was Yoko saying, "I didn't break up the Beatles." This is the April edition of Goldmine Magazine.

It's interesting because Yoko was really good about things. I sent her this photo many, many times for charities. And she would sign it and send it to charity auctions and things. I've never been able to get it on Rolling Stone. It's unfortunate, but that's life.

You've stayed in Baltimore your whole life. How has that influenced your photography?

Baltimore had good proximity to Washington [D.C.]. For a long time, Baltimore wasn't getting really good acts. In the last many years, U2 has been here, the Rolling Stones came a few years ago. For a little while I thought, 'Well, maybe I should move to New York.'

I got involved with a photo licensing company in New York called Star File. Star File was a photo agency where they would get you into events and then you would send them the photographs afterwards, and they would sell the photographs to various publications. But I didn't like that because what they really wanted were the kinds of photos of musicians that didn't want to be bothered.

Two other times they sent me out on job—and one of the times I didn't come back—one of them was a Sinatra show. And Sinatra was in Philly. [Star File] got me credentials; they got me in with the PR person. Sinatra had played in New York the day before and he was supposed to fly from New York to Philly. The airport was fogged over, so they had to drive him to Philly. I was standing backstage and Sinatra's car pulled up. I'll never forget, it was a long, blueish limousine. And he gets out of the car and immediately starts yelling at one of his guys.

And he says, "By the way, get that guy with the camera the '----' out of here!"

I could see he didn't want to be photographed. He didn't want to be bothered; he was in a horrible mood. He's wearing a denim jacket; he wore a toupee and his hair was messed up. So I told [Star File] the following day I couldn't get [the photos].

"Why couldn't you get it?"

60

I said, *"Because he was very agitated when he got out of his limo."*

"That's what we wanted! We wanted those photos."

So I said, *"I didn't get into photography to do busts."* *I really thought for a while, maybe I should move to New York. But, I realized this is a good place to be.*

People you loved to photograph?

John Lennon will always be my favorite. But B.B. King, the blues artist, right after John died . . . There was this great little venue called Painter's Mill Music Fair. See that picture there?

He points to the large framed photo of King.

It was February 1981. The guy who ran Painter's Mill, his name was Barry Heiserman. Barry was my first mentor. I had several.

Barry says, 'Why don't you come over and I'll introduce you to B.B. King. You can take some pictures and stuff.'

And he says, 'Bring that John Lennon picture with you.' Lennon died in December of '80, so this was just two months after John died.

[At the time], I was dating this young lady. I said, "Let's go see B.B. King."

She said, "Eh, he's a black guy."

"Yeah, but come on. It's great music. You'll have a great time."
We get there and she whispers to me: "We're the only white people here."

"It's fine, nobody's gonna bother you."

"I don't like this."

So we went and watched the show, and I had my credentials for photographing him. You probably shouldn't bring a date with you while you're working. As soon as the lights come up, she says, "Take me home!"

I said, "No, we're going to meet him, we're going backstage."

She says, "Take me home, get me out of here!"

I took her home and dropped her off at her house. Needless to say, I never went out with her again. And I drove right back [to Painter's Mill]. I pull up and locked my keys in my car. So I walk in backstage and Barry introduces me to B.B. King's manager. His name was Bebop.

I said to Barry, "Is there a phone nearby? I'm going to call my father."

Bebob said, "Why're going to call your father?"

"Cause I locked my keys in my car."

He says, "It's one o'clock in the morning. You going to call your father?"

"Yeah."

He says, "You don't have to do that." He goes over to one of those real big guys and he says, "Get this guy his keys out of his car for me." The [guy] has this [thin], long tool and puts it in the car and pulls the keys out.

Then they take me back into this room where's there's at least fifty people in this little, little room. B.B. King's sitting in the middle having his picture taken. He's talking with everybody. And he sees Barry standing next to me, and he sees Bebop.

As the room started to empty out, he says, "Hang on a minute because I want to talk with you." And one by one people are leaving this room until all of a sudden it's just he and I. And he says, "What's happening with you?"

I show him the photo of John and Yoko. He says, "I never met John Lennon, but John used to call me up and ask me about blues music. This is a great photo, can I have it?"

I said, "Sure."

I took a couple photos of him. I would say not every time he came back into town since then, [but] over a twenty year or so period, I probably photographed him maybe fifteen more times.

Last year B.B. King passed away, but about four years before he died, I made a collage of photos for him. I had it framed for him. Karen [Stuart's wife] and I went to see him at the Lyric Theater. At the end of the show, we went backstage and I gave him all these photos and he said, "People have taken my photo many, many times over the years. Nobody has ever given me anything like this before."

He turns to Karen and he goes, "You've got a good guy here. You've got a keeper here."

I think out of all the people I've photographed over the years, and met backstage, and got to have a nice rapport with, I think B.B. King is the one that I probably got to know the best.

Who Are You?

Stuart Zolotorow

Favorite Band: The Beatles

Favorite Song: "Long Tall Sally" cover by The Beatles

I think now you can only get it on an album called Beatles Past Masters. The energy of that song . . . I've seen McCartney do it several times live and he's never captured the energy that's on that recording . . . Just listen to that. It's a great, screaming, rock 'n' roll song.

Why I relate to classic rock:
It was my generation. Now, there's so much noise. John Lennon was a spokesman against the war. People speak out against things now, but he was the first celebrity, the first rock 'n' roller who protested for peace. And everything he and Yoko did after they got married was for peace. Everything. That was their whole thing. And people like Crosby, Stills, Nash, and Young.

In the 1960s it was the Vietnam War. It was the consciousness [of the people], and we held [the musicians] up on a different plane because they were the spokespeople for our generation.

Where Do We Go Now?

"No matter what happens in the future, rock 'n' roll will save the world."

~Pete Townshend

It feels like the entire world stops when you place the needle on the edge of a record. Whether the first note is an echoing blast, a gentle murmur, or simply a gracious hello, everything else seems to fade as the record moves round and round, flowing into the next track. When the needle clicks and the record ends, it's best to run your fingers over the small grooves, to feel physically the length and power of each song as much as you had just heard it.

Think of the longing in "Sloop John B;" the backward rush of psychedelic jazz in "Feel Flows." These Beach Boys songs surround the listener with sound waves that can be seen and heard and felt, stretching and expanding into the sky. Think of Bad Company, "The Way I Choose." Paul Rogers will cry with you: *"I don't need nobody to tell me the reason why/ If I only love you, baby/ I'll be satisfied."*

And yet, in recent years, fans are finding themselves more alone than ever. The year 2016 marked the deaths of legends: David Bowie and Glenn Frey of The Eagles, the former who showed the world the power of being alien under star-bound electric stage lights, the latter who invited us into sun patches and quiet living, questioning, and why-nots. Then, to follow, we lost Paul Kanter of Jefferson Airplane; both Keith Emerson and Greg Lake of Emerson, Lake & Palmer; Danny Smith of The Box Tops; Thunderclap Newman; Chris Squire of Yes; and King of Blues B.B King. There are rumors Eric Clapton might be retiring for good. Eric *Clapton*. Black Sabbath has already finished their last tour.

It's as though the once immortal giants of rock are fading, stepping down one by one, their exotic demeanors falling to the mundanity of old age. One can't help but wonder what will happen to rock 'n' roll? What has already happened? It's true that 2016 is a far cry from 1976. And as times change, clothes change, kids change, so do music soundtracks that mark time. Mainstream music today, while valid, comes from roots other than rock 'n' roll. The sound of rock 'n' roll might be a vintage lullaby, used as nostalgia, most oftentimes, rather than for listening.

Some argue, is it really so bad? The past is the past. We remember, but move on, welcoming new insights and rhythms that make us tick. But rock 'n' roll is so much more than just an arrangement of instruments. It was and *is* a culture, a lifestyle. It's a fist raised high above a crowd, symbolizing a movement. It's words everyone knows and sings together because they mean something larger than themselves. It's a cry for help, a plea for insanity, a quiet lament, an act of freedom. It's what gathered hundreds of thousands. In a world gearing desperation for individuality, rock 'n' roll is a reminder that we can live together, too, that the world is bigger than us and that's okay.

Rock 'n' roll was one of the first to break through race barriers, and it helped close the final door on segregation. It was a stampede against war and a reminder that we as a people are more than just a government. It is etched into history, hell, it helped *paint* history. Vietnam is remembered through the anger of "Fortunate Son," the desperation of "We Gotta Get Out of This Place," the terror of "Ohio."

It's clear rock 'n' roll has served a larger purpose many times over, and yet, it is still an extremely personal experience. Everyone understands it slightly different, feels the pulse in a different vein. Still, some people cling to it, caught in fear for the day someone like Keith Richards dies, the walking pharmacy who everyone believes will live forever (Joke: every time you smoke a cigarette, an hour is taken off of your life and given to Keith Richards; or, what kind of a future are we going to be leaving for Keith Richards). We wonder about when John Fogerty will leave, when Robert Plant will go silent. Like Don McLean, imagine the day the music truly dies, and wonder who will remember rock 'n' roll?

The music is still out there, thriving in underground patches, lingering in the dust of record stores and night clubs, wandering through the streets of blues, pounding in the chests of people who will never forget that feeling of being young and awakened for the first time. But, these people are growing older. If time were a record, rock 'n' roll would be sitting on the B Side right now, inching toward its ending track.

Take AC/DC for example. They're loud, unfiltered, lawless. They're a haze of anarchic guitar riffs, sexual innuendo, and schoolboy uniforms. They're considered one of the greatest hard rock bands to ever walk (no, *own*) the earth, and the coming years could be their end as we know it.

For almost forty-four years, AC/DC has reigned as an international symbol of rebellion. Carrying an album underarm, or wearing a t-shirt donning the iconic letters broken by a crackling lightning slash, anyone can profess a "stick it to the man" message. The music bridges generations and transcends age. Anthems like "Hell's Bells" and "Back in Black" will be recognizable to pretty much anyone. Some might find it miraculous that over forty years later, people still understand that language. And yet.

As speculations arise, rumors of the band calling it quits for good more serious than ever, there's good reason to wonder if this is the end of an era.

In the early years, AC/DC had its fair share of luck getting started. Malcolm and Angus' older brother, George, already experienced moderate fame with his 1960s pop group, The Easybeats. Both Malcolm and Angus took up guitar, but practiced separately. It wasn't until Malcolm thought to start his own group that he noticed his then-fifteen year old brother's talent and potential. It

68

was their sister who suggested Angus wear his school uniform—AC/DC's signature look. The brothers also snatched the band's name from a setting on her sewing machine that, well, had a nice ring to it, they thought.

Even securing their first lead singer, Bon Scott, was a lucky break. Malcolm noticed Scott in the crowd during one of their earliest concerts at the Largs Pier Hotel. Having recognized him in the local music scene, and aware of his voice, Malcolm jumped on the opportunity after the show. With Scott, AC/DC would go on to release seven platinum selling albums, including *High Voltage*, *Dirty Deeds Done Dirt Cheap*, and *Highway to Hell*. And when Scott died from alcohol poisoning in 1980, the transition for his replacement, Brian Johnson, was natural. Their first album without Scott, *Back in Black*, was also their most critically-acclaimed record, and the sixth bestselling record in American chart history.

But for the past three years, AC/DC's luck has started running dry. Drummer Phil Rudd was arrested for a second time. Malcolm Young was forced to retire, his early onset dementia and growing list of health complications too intense to ignore. Then, during the start of the band's Rock or Bust tour in 2014, Brian Johnson admitted to serious hearing loss, the risk too great to continue performing with the group. And finally, in September 2016, bassist Cliff Williams, who had joined in 1977, confirmed his quiet retirement.

Angus has worked relentlessly to recover AC/DC from its downward spiral. Angus told Rolling Stone magazine, "I feel obligated to keep it going, maybe because I was there in the beginning with him." When Malcolm retired, he made Angus promise to keep the band together. Stevie Young, Angus and Malcolm's nephew, replaced Malcolm on the rhythm guitar. And Axl Rose, lead singer for Guns N' Roses, filled in for Brian Johnson during the Rock or Bust Tour. When it comes to AC/DC's future, uncertainty is the only thing that's clear:

"We were committed to finishing the tour. Who knows what I'll feel after?" said Angus.

While there has been no confirmations for an official band retirement, the rumors continue to circulate. And the truth is, we're scared. We're all scared. What does the end of an era really mean? Can rock 'n' roll actually die? No one believed we would ever be faced with such a question, but the implications are more real than ever. And yet.

AC/DC once stood on a stage and told the world: "*For those about to rock, we salute you,*" as though reminding us that when it comes to music, we're all in it together, that rock 'n' will never be just a phase. That as long as the music exists it's alive.

In Baltimore, that's especially clear. On stations like 100.7 The Bay Baltimore's Classic Rock, the music is a constant, ready for the thousands who tune in each day. Record stores like Record and Tape Traders still carry the goods. We can only hope people will always be lining up, keeping the music as alive as it's ever been.

Have a Baltimore classic rock story of your own?

Visit *facebook.com/Baltimorerocknroll*

Resources

Andersen, Christopher P. *Mick: The Wild Life and Mad Genius of Jagger*. Detroit: Thorndike, 2012. Print.

Arrows, Days Of Broken. "Various Artists - WKTK Presents Baltimore's Best Rock (1978)." *Days of Broken Arrows*. N.p., 01 Jan. 1970.

"The Baltimore Experience African American Heritage Baltimore's Black History." *Baltimore National Heritage Area*. Web. 2017.

Billboard Magazine 11 Dec. 1971: n. pag. Print.

Burger, Jim. "The Hieronimus Code." *Baltimore Magazine*. N.p., 12 Aug. 2016.

Goldstein, Jessica. "On 'Hairspray's' 25th Anniversary, 'Buddy Deane' Committee Looks Back." *The Washington Post*. WP Company, 18 Jan. 2013.

Grimm, Bob. "The Woodstock Light Bus." *Bob Grimm's Woodstock Experience*. 2017.

Hieronimus, Bob. "Why I Paint Automobiles." *Woodstock Bus and Hieronimus' Painted Car Series*. 2017.

"History of the Germans in Baltimore." *World Heritage Encyclopedia*. 2017.

"History of the Poles in Baltimore." *World Heritage Encyclopedia*. 2017.

""Light" the Woodstock 1969 Bus from Hieronimus & Co., Inc." *Woodstock Bus*. N.p., Aug. 2016.

"Maryland Historical Society." *Maryland Historical Society*. 2017.

Miller, Jim. *The Rolling Stone Illustrated History of Rock & Roll, 1950-1980*. N.p.: Random House, 1980. Print.

"Not Quite as Popular as Jesus." *The Beatles Bible*. 2017.

Pollard, Kelvin, and Paola Scommenga. "Just How Many Baby Boomers Are There?" *Population Reference Bureau*. 2017.

Roll Hall of Fame and Museum Library and Archives. 2017.

"Rolling Stones US Tour 1969." *Rolling Stones Tours*. 2017.

Schoettler, Carl. "Where Jazz Still Echoes." *The Baltimore Sun*. 08 Dec. 2002.

"Singing Societies." *German Marylanders*.

Spangler, Jay. "John Lennon Interview: Larry Kane, Baltimore 9/13/1964." *Bealtes Interviews*. 2017.

Warden, Tim. "Radio Survey Records Charts." *ARSA THE AIRHEADS RADIO SURVEY ARCHIVE*. 2017.

"The Who Concert Guide." *The Who Tour Archive Live*. 2017.

Acknowledgments

My worst nightmare was once reality for then 18-year-old music journalist Cameron Crowe. In 1975, Crowe cracked Neil Young's notorious silence with an interview for Rolling Stone. While the feature piece eventually landed Crowe a permanent job with the magazine, the assignment wasn't easy. Young ended up talking to Crowe for so long, Crowe ran out of tapes. Young had to give him already filled cassettes with old song demos to record on top. While things worked out in the end, my heart breaks for Crowe every time I imagine him interrupting the interview to confess his problem.

I am eternally grateful to the recorder that never failed me, my trusted pen and paper, and of course, the generous people who helped me along the way and let me listen to their stories: Stephen Oshins, Professor Andrew Kellett, Stuart Zolotorow, Patricia Danoff, Alan Fink, Bob Cicero, Allison Fisher, Bob Hieronimous, Tom Carrico, Donna Jean Rumbley, Record and Tape Traders, and more. I am thankful to my editor, Mr. John Lewis, and my teacher, Mrs. Suzanne Supplee, who were there every step of the way, as enthusiastic about my topic as I am if not more. I also owe much to my Literary Arts Class of 2017. Every time I faltered, doubted, and stood back, you said "Rock on."

About the Author

Rebecca Schuman is a record collector and an avid fan of rock 'n' roll. Her work has been featured in the newspaper, *Catalyst*, and literary magazine, *Synergy* and has been recognized by the Scholastic Art and Writing competition. Outside of school, Schuman is an assistant art teacher. Her favorite songs at the moment include "Crimson and Clover" by Tommy James and the Shondells and "Almost Cut My Hair" by Crosby, Stills, Nash, and Young. She owns over 120 original vinyl records, which makes it difficult to choose favorites. In fall 2017, she will be attending Drew University in New Jersey.

48680161R00048

Made in the USA
San Bernardino, CA
02 May 2017